FIN'S SWIM

21
DAYS
on the
FRASER
RIVER

FIN'S SWIM

HELEN O'BRIAN

illustrated by
DEBBIE BOWLES

ACKNOWLEDGEMENTS

My first thanks are to Cole Harris and Michael Church for introducing me to the middle Fraser on a trip in 2004 and to Rick Blacklaws, also on that trip, for sowing the seed for me of getting youth on the river. Thank you Fin Donnelly for inspiring and making this book possible and all the 'Fraseriffics' who were so helpful, especially Darwin and Susan Baerg. Thanks also to David Stephens for his editorial assistance, to Stacey Noyes for design and to Debbie Bowles for the illustrations. And to readers, conversationalists and others who contributed: Ann Johnston, Bette Hawes, Marian McLean, Sally Sexsmith, Lael Whitehead, Sally Ireland, David Alexander, Kit Pearson, Phyllis Simon, Judith Steedman, Valerie Somerville, my husband John and our daughters, Melanie, Amy and Meghan.

Published by Hatake Press

622 Gallagher Bay Road, Mayne Island, BC, V0N 2J2 Canada

www.finsswim.ca

Printed and bound in Canada by Friesens

LIBRARY AND ARCHIVES CANADA CATALOGUING IN PUBLICATION

O'Brian, Helen, 1947-

Fin's swim : 21 days on the Fraser River / Helen O'Brian ; illustrated by Debbie Bowles.

Includes bibliographical references.

ISBN 978-0-9881042-0-4

1. Donnelly, Fin--Travel--British Columbia--Fraser River--Juvenile literature. 2. Swimming--British Columbia--Fraser River--Juvenile literature. 3. Natural history--British Columbia--Fraser River--Juvenile literature. 4. Fraser River (B.C.)--History--Juvenile literature. 5. Fraser River (B.C.)--Description and travel--Juvenile literature. I. Bowles, Debbie, 1962- II. Title.

FC3817.4.O27 2013   j917.11'3044   C2012-907406-3

For Fin and the Fraser

FROM A LETTER FIN WROTE FOLLOWING HIS SWIM

I thought further of my swim last year. One could easily argue that, like the pioneers of Canada, I conquered the river by swimming it — I beat it, controlled it and overcame it. But that is not how I look at it at all. I swam with the river – I learned to work with it, using its characteristics and nature to my advantage. I learned to respect its power, I saw its beauty and I experienced its sustenance. I developed a relationship with the river – it was a powerful experience. And I learned quite quickly not to abuse that relationship as my health depended on its health.

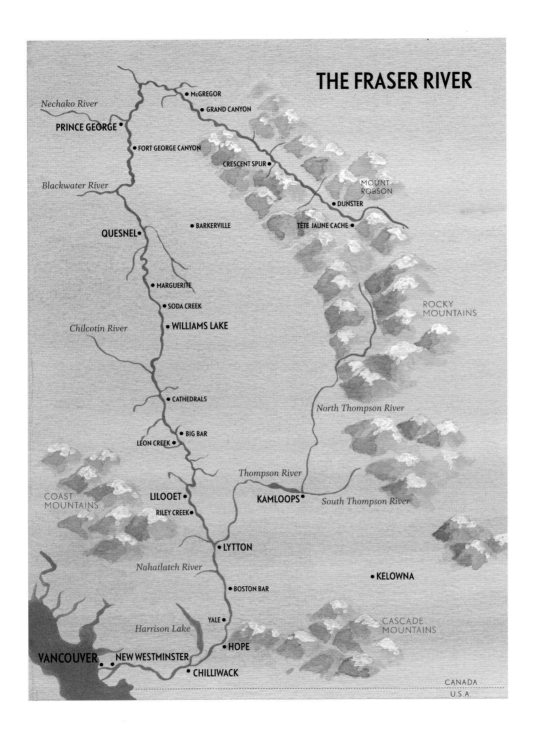

THE FRASER RIVER

Nechako River

• McGREGOR

• GRAND CANYON

PRINCE GEORGE •

• FORT GEORGE CANYON

CRESCENT SPUR •

Blackwater River

MOUNT ROBSON

• DUNSTER

QUESNEL •

• BARKERVILLE

TÊTE JAUNE CACHE •

• MARGUERITE

• SODA CREEK

ROCKY MOUNTAINS

Chilcotin River

• **WILLIAMS LAKE**

• CATHEDRALS

North Thompson River

• BIG BAR

LEON CREEK •

Thompson River

COAST MOUNTAINS

LILOOET •

RILEY CREEK •

KAMLOOPS •

South Thompson River

• **LYTTON**

Nahatlatch River

• **KELOWNA**

• BOSTON BAR

YALE •

Harrison Lake

CASCADE MOUNTAINS

VANCOUVER •

• **HOPE**

• **NEW WESTMINSTER**

• **CHILLIWACK**

CANADA

U.S.A.

CONTENTS

RIVER

In the beginning River was just a glacial trickle bubbling out of a crevice high up in the Rocky Mountains. It was so pure and innocent as it cascaded northwards, gathering in more trickles and rivulets along the way and gradually growing larger, its icy waters running faster. Eventually River flowed into Moose Lake set in a deep valley surrounded by mountains so high they almost touched the sky. Little fish and water spiders moved down the lake with River, carefully avoiding the dragonflies that swooped low looking for food. A grizzly bear and her cubs explored the underbrush at the water's edge, searching for berries and roots. When River reached the far northwest end of the long narrow lake it spilled out and continued on its long journey downhill. It rapidly became much bigger, boiling and roaring along until it poured over Overlander Falls. In the pool below, River encountered its first Chinook salmon, all battered and misshapen at the end of its long spawning journey. Two eagles soared overhead waiting to feed on the carcass. To the north, the great Mount Robson towered high above the trees looking south over Mount Terry Fox. Moving beyond these two stone giants, River raced over Rearguard Falls into a valley that gradually opened up, allowing River to expand and meander along at a more leisurely pace. Suddenly, there was a very BIG splash as something broke through River's surface. It was larger than any fish River had ever seen. A big shadow with a contraption at one end that made River's water swirl and foam soon joined this mysterious object. What indeed was River to make of this bizarre intrusion? With 1,400 kilometers to travel before it reached the Pacific Ocean, River accepted that it would have company on its long journey.

TÊTE JAUNE CACHE to PRINCE GEORGE

UPPER FRASER

For the descent of a river is a journey
through time as well as space,
through history and culture as well
as through landscape.

RICHARD BOCKING
MIGHTY RIVER

THE FIRST DAY

With a loud excited holler twenty-nine year old Fin Donnelly leapt into the Fraser River. The day was sunny and warm, but the shock of the glacial waters momentarily took his breath away. Outfitted in a green and black wetsuit with matching hood, black gloves and flippers, swimming goggles and an orange life jacket, Fin took the first strokes of his very long swim down the mighty Fraser River. His support raft followed close behind, carrying the Fraseriffics — a crew of four plus Captain Darwin — and all their gear. The big motor on the back churned quietly as the raft moved out into the river.

As a competitive swimmer Fin had come close to making the Canadian Olympic team before he decided to use his athletic skills to bring attention to the health and preservation of the natural environment. He had already done fourteen marathon swims but nothing nearly as long as the Fraser.

It was late summer in 1995 and Fin had been planning this day for over a year, the beginning of his swim for the salmon and for the life of the river. He was swimming the Fraser not for his own glory but to bring attention to the health of the river and to all the life it supports. He knew that the number of salmon returning to spawn each year was rapidly declining and thought it might be a warning similar to the canary in the coal mine that dies when the air becomes too poisonous to support human life.

Almost 200 years earlier, in 1808, Simon Fraser and his crew of twenty-three men had traveled the river from Prince George, hoping to find a navigable trade route to the Pacific Ocean. Where the river was too dangerous, they had been forced to travel overland. Fin planned to swim as much of the river as he possibly could and ride through the treacherous sections on the raft with Darwin and the crew.

Fin's first plunge took place at Tête Jaune Cache, a two-store town near the base of Mount Terry Fox and not far from British Columbia's border with Alberta. T-Jean, as the locals call it, is the place where the Fraser River widens out after bursting from its source high in the Rocky Mountains. From T-Jean the river slowly zigzags its way northwest through the Robson Valley and the Rocky Mountain Trench before turning south to Hope and then west out to the coast.

Here, in its upper reaches the Fraser runs slowly in late summer, bubbling over shallow gravel bars that provide perfect spawning grounds for the migrating Chinook salmon at the end of their long journey. Its water is a milky turquoise, coloured by 'rock flour' from glacial streams and creeks feeding into it. Some of this glacial silt ends up on the rich farmlands of the Lower Fraser Valley and some travels with the river, like Fin and the young salmon, all the way down to the Fraser Delta where it empties into the Pacific Ocean.

Fin spotted a big bald eagle flying above him as he swam and recalled the words of a young native woman he knew. She had told him that before her grandfather left this world he had promised her that whenever she asked for his protection he would appear in the form of a soaring eagle. Fin quietly hoped the great bird would watch over him for the next twenty-one days on the river.

Magnified through his goggles, Fin could see the majestic but battered and roe-heavy salmon swimming upstream beneath him, about to spawn, about to die. As his hand gently brushed the back of a passing Chinook he immediately felt at one with the river and thought how curious it was that the fish were ending their journey just as he was beginning his.

Fin learned a lot about the river in those first hours of swimming, mostly by trial and error. In this upper section the river runs shallow in late summer, but there are some deep channels carved out by the current. To avoid the wide sweeps of the meandering river, Fin tried swimming the shortest route through the channels closest to the inside banks. To his surprise and dismay, however, the back eddying current actually worked against him. While the spawning salmon could use these eddies to their advantage as they moved upstream, the currents dictated that Fin had to swim where the returning fish did not.

Gravel bars could usually be spotted up ahead by the white rippling water bouncing over them. Darwin and the crew were always on the lookout for these and more dangerous spots, but one went unnoticed. With a thud, Fin suddenly found himself grounded. Straightening up, he began to walk, flippers flapping across the river-smoothed stones, a momentary relief from swimming. Already his muscles felt strained and overworked, but the respite was brief and he was soon back in the water.

Turning his head for air on every third or fourth stroke, Fin had a rhythmical view of low willow-covered banks punctuated by towering cottonwood trees. He saw eagles and osprey scanning the river for their next meal, a deer resting on a dry gravel bar and the odd hungry kingfisher sweeping the water. When he saw cows down by the river he knew the landscape beyond would soon open up to hay and grain fields. Once, up ahead, Fin saw a long rat-like tail flash and disappear. Then, a few seconds later, up popped the whiskered face of a river otter only five or six meters in front of him. More curious than surprised, the otter stayed up to watch as this odd creature stroked closer before duck-diving back under.

That first day was particularly long and uneventful. The river gently meandered as Fin stroked with the current, the raft always nearby. As the minutes and hours ticked by, Fin grew wearier and colder. His mind seemed a little fuzzy, a little confused. He wondered if he might be on the verge of hypothermia. After all, the temperature of the water at T-Jean had been just 10 degrees Celsius when he started out, and it would certainly not have warmed up yet.

Stroke . . . Stroke . . . He just had to keep going. He had to make it through this first grueling day. He had to do it for the salmon… Stroke… Stroke… He imagined the feel of strong fingers massaging his tired and knotted muscles. He thought about his cozy sleeping bag. He thought about what he might have for dinner—perhaps a big bowl of hot pasta with tomato sauce topped with grated cheese… Stroke… Stroke… Keep going. The friendly sounds of the crew singing and

chatting nearby warmed his spirit if not his body. He could do it.

Fin had been in the water for seven hours and was getting really tired. Around each long elbow bend in the river he expected to see the Dunster Flower Bridge marking the end of the first day's swim. But, as the sun dropped lower in the western sky and there was no bridge in sight he began to worry that he might have to stop earlier than planned. Another long hour passed before a loud cheer came from the raft, followed by an even louder one from an excited gathering of Dunsterites waving from the Flower Bridge. With a great sigh of relief, Fin swam the last little distance knowing he had successfully completed Day One of his epic swim. Perhaps, he thought, the hardest day of all, but that remained to be seen.

DOWN THE RIVER

Day Two dawned fine and warm, but Fin's body was racked by aches and pains. In spite of a soothing massage the night before as well as months of training, he still felt every second, every minute, every stroke, of the first day's eight-hour icy swim. The skin on his shoulders and underarms was very tender even though, when ordering his wetsuit, he had taken great care to make sure the inner seams were smooth. An uncomfortable rash had appeared and his muscles ached. He had an abrasion on his heel and his neck was quickly being rubbed raw. Discomfort aside, he had to get back in the water. Inspired by all thirty of the Dunster school children who had come to see him off, Fin took the plunge and set out again

He knew that the swim from Dunster to Prince George would take several long days. The river's wandering nature made the distance it traveled from T-Jean to Prince George twice that of the highway route. In fact, it would take Fin seven days to swim what a car could drive in a mere four or five hours. At this point Fin could swim faster than the raft could float but Darwin was confident that this part of the river was smooth and safe enough for Fin to take the lead. Later in the trip the raft would always be in front, the crew constantly checking the river for any lurking dangers.

There was no traffic on the quiet river. Other than the raft, there was not another boat, kayak or canoe to be seen. From time to time Fin heard a train rumbling along the nearby C.N. tracks or the throaty sound of a transport van on the Yellowhead Highway running parallel to the river or the sound of a tractor in the fields or the buzz of a chainsaw. And occasionally the cry of an eagle or the deep croak of a Great Blue Heron broke through the sound of the laughing waters.

Each time a tributary emptied into the Fraser, Fin could feel the current strengthen. Turquoise glacial waters from the Raush, the Holmes, the Dore, the McKale, the Goat and other mountain streams slowly blended into the Fraser which became increasingly murky as it picked up mud from eroding banks and runoff from farms and logging operations. On the distant hillsides Fin saw evidence of clear cutting. It looked like a giant patchwork quilt in shades of green and brown stitched together by logging roads.

Along the riverbanks fireweed was still in bloom as well as asters and the occasional harebell. Near the shore, old wooden pylons, once used as tie-ups for steamships, poked out of the water like soldiers standing at attention. Before the Grand Trunk Pacific Railroad was completed in 1914, sternwheelers had moved both goods and people up and down the Fraser from Prince George to T-Jean.

At Crescent Spur Fin was met by a group of local environmentalists who had invited him to dedicate an historic plaque. Still in his wetsuit he was taken

by motorcycle to the head of the Goat River Trail where the unveiling of the plaque took place. It is an old trail that was once a well-worn trade route for native peoples and later was used by Europeans traveling between the Upper Fraser, Barkerville and the Bowron Lakes. The area is rich in old growth forest, an important grizzly and mountain caribou habitat as well as spawning grounds for salmon, but logging and other human activities were posing an imminent threat. By emphasizing both its historical and environmental importance, these concerned citizens were attempting to protect this wilderness area and keep the trail open for hiking only. Fin was pleased to play a part.

Back in the river thoughts of the disappearing mountain caribou filled Fin's head. He had learned that 80% of the mountain caribou's winter diet is old man's beard, a lichen that only grows on old growth trees. It seemed hard to believe that these big animals could survive the winter on something that looked as if it had very little nutritional value, cleverly using the deep hard packed snow as a natural ladder to reach the high lichen-covered branches. He had also learned that road building and logging activities were removing not only the caribou's precious food sources but making access easy for their chief predator, the wolf. And with the opening up of old growth forests, helicopters, skiers, snowmobilers and hunters posed further threats to the already endangered caribou. Stroke by stroke Fin was realizing that the scope of his swim was moving well beyond the waters of the mighty Fraser to include life in the many watersheds feeding into it.

THE GRAND CANYON

Five days into the swim Fin woke to brilliant sun, but much to his surprise the river below the campsite was entirely blanketed in dense fog. All he could see was the pole of the raft's sun umbrella along with the tops of some scrubby willows jutting skywards above the thick mist. The sound of the sleepy hidden river whispered mysteriously below. Marking time was all that Fin and the others could do that morning.

While waiting for the fog to lift Fin imagined the day ahead of him. He knew this was the day he would travel through the Grand Canyon Rapids, the most treacherous waters on the Upper Fraser. Until now the river had been manageable but these rapids were a different story. Fin had read about the Overlanders, an intrepid group of travelers who had made their way across the

country by foot, wagon, horse and boat heading for the Cariboo and its gold in 1862. Near what is now Tête Jaune Cache the group had split, the majority of them choosing the Fraser River route and the rest trekking overland to the Thompson River. All went well for the Fraser group until they came to the Grand Canyon where they lost ten canoes and three men.

Fin recalled the story of one of the Overlanders, a man named Carpenter. Before attempting to travel through the canyon, Carpenter and his two companions, Alexander and Jones, surveyed the churning water from the cliffs above, looking for the best route. On seeing the frightening sight below them, Carpenter must have felt certain he would never survive. Before setting out in their two dugouts lashed together, Alexander had noticed Carpenter taking a moment to write in his notebook. He then saw him put the notebook back in the pocket of his coat which he removed and hung on the bough of a tree. Alexander and Jones somehow made it through the canyon but they never saw Carpenter again. Remembering Carpenter's coat, Alexander walked back up around the canyon to retrieve it. In the notebook Carpenter had written, "Arrived this day at the canyon at 10 am and drowned running the canoe down. God keep my poor wife!"*

When the fog finally lifted, the river awaited Fin once again. While the others were busy loading the raft, he suited up and did his stretches and warm-ups before plunging into the water. This day, like the preceding days, began with the river gently and monotonously snaking its way through the pastoral Rocky Mountain Trench. Stroking into the late afternoon, it seemed inconceivable to Fin that such treacherous waters as he had read about would soon appear beyond one of the sweeping curves up ahead. He noticed a pair of eagles perched in a tree at the river's edge and silently asked them to keep a safe watch over him.

The raft was in front of Fin and the team aboard were carefully watching the water ahead. Before too long they began to hear the roar of the canyon and quickly circled back to get Fin onto the raft. Steamships may once have successfully navigated these rapids but Fin would not. He did not want to end up like Mr. Carpenter.

All their gear was well secured and their life jackets tightened. Fin and the others braced themselves and took a firm hold of the tight ropes attached to the raft. With the guiding help of the powerful motor and the experienced hand of Darwin at the helm, the raft raced ahead through the roiling waters of the Grand Canyon. At a sharp left turn where the water runs fastest and is most ferocious, the rubber raft was thrown against the canyon wall but bounced off

* Richard C. Bocking, *Mighty River: a portrait of the Fraser* (Vancouver: Douglas & McIntyre, 1997), 34.

with no ill effects to it or its occupants. Had they been in a dugout canoe, a raft of cottonwood logs or a timbered steamboat they might not have been so lucky!

In a quiet backwater below the canyon the team made camp on a lovely gravel beach. From the shore it was remarkable to watch the spawning Chinook salmon leaping into the air in preparation for the canyon's white water challenge. Those that made it all the way up to T-Jean would try to make it over Rearguard Falls just beyond the town. If successful, they would then meet an impassable wall of water at Overlander Falls marking the end of their last journey.

ON TO
PRINCE GEORGE

No blanket of fog would slow down the start to Day Six. As the sun rose into a clear blue sky, Fin struggled into his cold and damp wetsuit wondering if he would ever get used to this uncomfortable clammy beginning to each morning. Ten push-ups, four spinal twists, six forward bends followed by six side bends, a few arm windmills, ten calming deep breaths and then . . . into the river. Only two more days to Prince George.

The Grand Canyon had been thrilling, providing a taste of the famous white waters that lay ahead, but for now the river had returned to its all too familiar tedious self. Stroke by stroke Fin continued on down the long winding river. He was grumpy and tired. The regular breaks for a warm drink, an energy bar and half a banana provided a necessary rhythm to the long days. To counter the monotony he silently sang old songs, struggling to remember all the words or he ran through his repertoire of river jokes with good punch lines. Anything to help pass the time.

Over the next two days Fin swam past Sinclair Mills, past Dewey, under the trestle bridge at McGregor and on past Hansard. At Upper Fraser he had his first encounter with sawmill pollution. Small islands of scummy yellow froth floated on the surface and a sharp scent filled his nostrils. The water that inevitably seeped into his mouth had an unpleasant bitterness to it. The river was no longer pure and innocent.

He swam past the mouths of the McGregor River and the Herring River. He swam the first half of the Giscome Rapids. He swam past the little community of Shelley on the outskirts of Prince George and then past the confluence of the Nechako River, feeling a surge of energy as it emptied into the Fraser.

When Fin finally reached Fort George Park, he was very tired but overjoyed by the welcoming cheers of the waiting crowd. As he clambered ashore everyone wanted to shake his hand, give him a hug, thank him for what he was doing and offer him words of encouragement.

In seven days Fin had completed the first third of his long swim, perhaps the easiest part of the journey. On the other hand, it might have been the most difficult because of the long tediously plodding days of endless stroking through the gentle landscape. Tonight he was looking forward to a hot shower, a massage for his aching muscles, a hearty meal and a good long sleep.

Day Eight was scheduled as a rest day in Prince George—a rest from swimming that is! Fin spent most of the day speaking to reporters, doing radio interviews, talking with students at the university, meeting the mayor of Prince George, being the guest speaker at the Rotarian's lunch, riding in taxis and generally dealing with the hustle and bustle of the city. Instead of being the day of rest his body so desperately needed it had been exhausting.

Fin went to bed somewhat out of sorts. He felt like a fish out of water and looked forward to getting back into the river the next day, following the path of the great explorer Simon Fraser.

Simon Fraser's employer, the North West Company, had instructed him to follow what was thought to be the Columbia River in search of a navigable trade route to the Pacific. When Fraser and his men set out from Fort George, New Caledonia on May 28, 1808, the river was running high and fast with melting snow and seasonal runoff.

On this expedition Fraser and his men endured hardships unlike any they had previously experienced, taking thirty-five days to reach the Fraser delta and thirty-four to return. Theirs was one of the most grueling explorations recorded in the history of British Columbia and a test of extreme physical endurance.

JOURNAL

SATURDAY MAY 22 [28], 1808.

Having made every necessary preparation for a long voyage, we embarked at 5 o'clock, A.M. in four canoes, at Fraser's River [i.e., at the mouth of the Nechako River]. Our crew consisted of nineteen men, two Indians, Mr. Steward [Stuart], Mr. Quesnil [Quesnel]. And myself; in all twenty four. At this place [the] Columbia [i.e., the Fraser River] is about 300 yards wide. It overflows its banks, and has a very strong current.

Simon Fraser *Letters & Journals, 1806-1808*, ed. W. Kaye Lamb (Toronto: MacMillan, 1960), 61.

PRINCE GEORGE to YALE

MIDDLE FRASER

IN THE PATH
OF THE EXPLORERS

There was a hint of autumn crispness in the air and the morning was crystal clear at Fort George Park on Day Nine. Fin stood by the river not far from the spot where Simon Fraser and his men had set out that cold spring morning one hundred and eighty-seven years earlier. Shaking out the cobwebs from his 'day of rest', Fin struggled into his cold sandy wetsuit and ceremoniously poured river water over his head and body while turning to the four directions, asking the river to protect him. He would repeat this ritual every morning as he headed downstream into more dangerous waters on this north-south leg of his journey.

Fin was happy to be swimming again. As he left behind the sights, the sounds and the smells of the city he felt the tensions of the previous day fall away. An eagle soared above, one eye on the migrating salmon, the other on Fin. He stroked effortlessly with the stronger current past the muffled hum of industry shielded by trees on the riverbank. A belted kingfisher swooped down with a loud rattle in search of its breakfast.

The much talked about changing moods of the Fraser began to reveal themselves and it wasn't long before the river suddenly narrowed, squeezing the water between steep banks. On the raft ahead Darwin was guiding Fin through the rapids when an unexpected surge pulled him under and popped him up hard against a rock, momentarily stealing his breath away. With his heart pounding in his ears, another rush of white water just as quickly whisked him out beyond danger. Somewhat stunned, he signaled for a short break to regain his equilibrium and to make sure his wetsuit was still in tact.

A little further downstream Fin was only too happy to climb out onto the raft to pass through Fort George Canyon. He remembered reading that Simon Fraser had found these rapids menacing and extremely difficult to navigate, but once through he and his men had been rewarded with an abundance of wild onions that spiced their monotonous daily diet of pemmican. Fin closed his eyes and lifted his nose to the air, hoping for the pungent scent of onions but alas, it was too late in the season.

That evening, after a massage and a meal of pasta and vegetables, Fin took a stroll up the Blackwater River near where they were camped. It being late summer the river was low, leaving a wide sandy bank punctuated with stones rolled smooth by the roiling waters of spring run-off. A pile of fresh bear scat sent bristling goose bumps down his spine but, certain that any bear would be more interested in the salmon moving up the river than in him, Fin boldly carried on.

As he sat on a rock digging his bare toes into the cool sand, he contemplated the journey that the explorer Alexander Mackenzie had made up this same river in 1793 looking for a route to the Pacific. Suddenly, Fin's big toe hit something sharp. Searching with his hands he found a beautiful broken shell of a sort found on the coast, not 350 kilometers inland where he now sat. Back at camp Fin showed his find to the others, one of whom identified it as a dentalium shell. These slender shells resembling miniature elephant trunks were among the items native people of the Pacific Coast traded with the interior peoples. Another prized item from the coast was oolichan grease* which the traders carried in large wooden boxes across the rugged Coast Mountains. The weather and bugs were often horrendous and the footing bad. Inevitably some of the precious oolichan grease spilled from the boxes giving the name Grease Trails to these trading routes. It was known that a Carrier village had once stood near where Fin and the team were camped at the mouth of the Blackwater River and that this village marked the end of one of the most famous Grease Trails. Fin's shell was undoubtedly one of the coastal items that had been traded for buckskin, dried berries and other goods from the interior peoples.

Fin zipped the dentalium treasure carefully into his pocket and then tucked himself into his cozy sleeping bag, marveling at the many layers of history he was experiencing. He slept well that night.

---

* This smelly grease is rendered from the small oily fish called oolichan that once flourished on the coast. The oolichan is about the size and shape of a smelt. The fish were rendered into an edible grease that stored well and was used as a dietary supplement.

THE SINGING TREE

The swim on Day Ten was easy and the turbulent waters of Cottonwood Canyon safe enough at this time of year for Fin to bounce through. A big snaking bow in the river wearily reminded him of the unending meanders of his first few days on the river. How he wished he could grow wings and fly like an eagle in a straight line to Quesnel where he was scheduled to meet the mayor at noon.

The town of Quesnel sits on a rise of land where the river of the same name empties into the Fraser. In 1808 Simon Fraser referred to it in his journal as "Quesnel's river," naming it after Jules Maurice Quesnel, a twenty-two year old clerk of the North West Company and third in command of the expedition. Some fifty years later the town became the service centre for the great Cariboo

Gold Rush. Gold seekers, like the Overlanders, came downriver from the north and thousands more traveled up from the mouth of the Fraser by boat, on foot or on the backs of mules and horses. From Quesnel they turned east to the gold fields of Barkerville. Some made a fortune in the area but most returned home empty-handed while others found work and a new life out on the coast.

Members of the local canoe and kayak club met Fin a couple of kilometres above the town to escort him to the riverside landing and then, on foot, to the town centre. It felt so good to shed his swimming fins, his goggles, hood and gloves and to have the opportunity to stretch his legs and relax his weary arms. As they walked up the hill, a warm gentle breeze sighed rhythmically through the leafy branches of the big cottonwood trees along the riverbank. Fin stopped the little procession to listen more carefully. The sound from the trees had the regular beat of a song he had heard members of the Tsilhqot'in Nation sing when he had visited one of their communities. He had been told then that it was a very old song passed down through generations and was sung by five of their members who had been sent to the gallows in 1864 by the hanging judge Matthew Begbie. It was said that the five men sang until the footing was pulled out from under them and that even now they continue to sing. Fin began walking again as one of the escorts, seemingly out of the blue, began telling him the story of the 'singing cottonwoods.'

The group continued to make their way up from the river to meet with the mayor, a reporter from the Quesnel Advisor, river enthusiasts and curious passersby. Hotels and eateries lined the main street offering food and rest to tourists of a different sort than the earlier gold seekers. Those visiting Quesnel today are more likely in search of a souvenir than a fortune.

Back in the river again and filled with encouragement and accolades from the mayor and the people of Quesnel, Fin swam past one of the town's wood processing mills, a shaft of white smoke billowing skywards, the machines gently humming. As he stroked on with the current, now freshened by the additional waters from the Quesnel River, Fin saw eagles every time he turned his head for a breath. Some were perched in tree snags, others soared gracefully on an updraft or swooped down over the river in front of him, attracted by the migrating salmon. Fin knew this to be a healthy sign that meant there must be enough food for them and that they were managing to survive the ever-increasing encroachments of human activity and pollution.

That evening the team camped on a sandy island sitting low in the water, a straightforward run of about thirty kilometers downstream from Quesnel. A few years earlier Darwin recalled camping on the same island. He was amazed at how its shape had been completely altered by the river, depositing sand and silt in some places, carrying it away from others.

They pitched their tents and set up the kitchen on a sandy bank rippled and packed hard by the high water of other seasons. In the quiet shallows off the backside of the island a dozen or more Great Blue Herons on their long stilt legs were fishing for their dinner. All was peaceful around them, but that didn't soothe the growing pain in Fin's shoulder and the irritating rash on his back and arms.

WHITE WATER BEGINS

Fin woke early on Day Eleven to the sound of geese honking . . . again. On and off during the night he had heard them as he slept restlessly, trying to avoid lying on his aching shoulder. The geese must be on the move, just like him.

Fin knew this would be the last day of relatively easy swimming. Darwin had told him that south of Soda Creek the river would narrow, flow faster and be much more dangerous. The thought excited him but, for today, he would enjoy this calmer face of the Fraser.

Before pulling on his damp, sandy second skin he got help taping moleskin over his chafed shoulder and smearing a sticky white barrier cream on his rash. A generous slathering of Vaseline over most of his body completed his preparations.

The cool nights and warm days of late summer seemed to be a recipe for morning fog. Fin swam very close to the raft for the first hour, until the sun burned off all the mist. The banks were low, sculpted by the river, and just above them fields of hay were ripening for a second or maybe even a third harvest. Huge pulsating sprinklers drawing water up from the river kept the fields irrigated, the fine spray sparkling in the sunlight. Occasionally cows could be seen grazing on the stubble left from a recent cut.

At Alexandria, named after another explorer, Alexander Mackenzie, Fin and the crew stretched their legs with a walk up to the abandoned clapboard church built long ago by Catholic missionaries. Even in Mackenzie's day, this area had been an important crossroads and trading centre for First Nations peoples. It was here at Alexandria in 1793 that the local Carrier people, making alarming noises in their throats in imitation of the rage of the river ahead, convinced Mackenzie to return north to the Blackwater River and take the Grease Trail west in search of the Pacific Ocean.

Further downstream Fin swam past Marguerite where two towers stood on either side of the river, marking all that remained of the reaction ferry that used to cross there. A cable had once stretched between the towers and a small ferry, more like a platform on floats, was bridled to it and propelled across from one side to the other by the river's strong current. The ferry could only carry a couple of cars or trucks but it made a huge difference to the people who lived in the area.

After a good night's rest at their campsite a few kilometers south of Marguerite, Fin felt ready for the challenge of the white water that Darwin had raved about so much. Nevertheless, Day Twelve began gently with an easy swim down to Soda Creek, a little community that was once a bustling port serving the Fraser River steamships that operated out of Prince George. Soda Creek was as far south as the sternwheelers had been able to safely travel. It was also the northern end of the Cariboo Wagon Road where both goods and people had made the transfer from land to water or vice versa, depending on which direction they were traveling. The hotels, bars and stores that once served the lively town are all gone and now only a few farms remain, working the rich soil of the valley.

South of Soda Creek Fin swam under the bright orange Rudy Johnson Bridge built by a local farmer of the same name in 1968. Apparently farmer Johnson nearly lost his wife when she fell off the old Soda Creek reaction ferry. Tired of the ferry being the only river crossing for miles, Johnson was determined to build a bridge. The story goes that he found an abandoned bridge in Alaska, shipped 3,300 pieces of that bridge by barge and rail to nearby Williams Lake and then reassembled it on site. To help recover the costs, it operated as a toll bridge until the provincial government bought it in 1978.

At Russian Island the team pulled in for lunch with time to explore the abandoned tumbledown mining operation set up years ago by an industrious Russian prospector. What was left of his house was high up on the bluff above the pebble beach and nearby, a rusty old winch and cable, once used to haul everything up to the site, was still in place. Another even thicker cable was strung across to the mainland for the aerial tram that had once carried the miner and his supplies on and off the island.

That afternoon things began to change quite rapidly. Fin felt nervous butterflies well up in his stomach as the cliffs grew higher, the river narrower and the water flowed faster and whiter. The high banks shaded the river from the warmth of the sun but for Fin the sudden chill made no difference. He had already swum through four or five sets of rapids, hardly missing a stroke, and rafted through another three, but now Darwin circled back to pick him up once again. Chimney Creek Canyon loomed ahead, the rapids that Simon Fraser had attempted.

SIMON FRASER'S
JOURNAL

WEDNESDAY, JUNE 1, 1808.

I ordered the best five [men] out of the crews into a canoe lightly loaded. This [order] was no sooner given than obeyed; and the canoe in a moment was underway. After passing the first cascade the canoe lost her course, and was drawn to the eddy, where it was whirled about for a considerable time, and seemingly in suspense whether to sink or swim. The men had no power over her. However it took a favourable turn and by degrees was led from this dangerous vortex again in to the stream. It then continued flying from one danger to another, until the cascade near the last where in spite of every effort, the whirlpools forced it against a projecting rock, which happened to be a low point. Upon this the men disembarked, and saved their own lives, and contrived to save the property; for the greatest danger was still a head. Of course to continue on the water would be certain destruction.

Simon Fraser *Letters & Journals, 1806-1808*, ed. W. Kaye Lamb (Toronto: MacMillan, 1960), 68.

Fin felt safe on the raft as it rushed and bounced like a bucking bronco through the churning water between the steep cliffs. He held tight to the ropes secured along the side of the raft, enjoying himself thoroughly and watching the others get drenched with spray. Darwin, at the helm, wore a particularly satisfying grin. Whooping and hollering all the way, they were soon safely through and gently swirling in the eddies below.

What an exciting day it had been, ending with a delicious surprise at Sheep Creek Bridge where they made camp for the night. A small group of enthusiastic supporters from Williams Lake had driven out to greet them, bringing ice cream!

PETROGYLPHS AND STORM CLOUDS

It was a long night for everyone. Giant logging trucks, heading east to the mills near Williams Lake, rumbled heavily across the Sheep Creek Bridge. Once on the other side they slowly climbed the steep switchback, their gears screeching and grinding with every shift. Empty trucks with their piggy-backed trailers hungry for more logs, rattled across the bridge in the opposite direction. And, just to make sure their presence was noticed by the campers below, some of the drivers gave their air horns a friendly blast.

Fin woke that morning to the smell of bacon cooking accompanied by the sound of swatting and cursing. The rising sun was just beginning to warm the campsite and with it came the wasps. The hungry pests were everywhere, both defending their colony and searching for protein. It was the bacon they really wanted, but in their voracious madness they attacked the walking protein as well. Darwin was the first to be bitten as he loudly cursed their bad luck in setting up camp near a sleeping wasps nest.

Within twenty minutes the team broke camp and loaded everything on to the raft, including the well-covered bacon. Fin managed to suit up without getting stung and quickly did his stretches. He took particular care with his ritual water ceremony, asking the river to protect him, especially after this beginning. Into the river he went, the raft close beside him. About half an hour later, certain they were beyond wasp range, Fin was hauled out for his pest-free breakfast of fruit and granola while the others enjoyed the bacon!

The river ran swiftly that morning. As Fin stroked rhythmically from one swirling eddy to another Darwin watched with admiration. It was such a beautiful sight, as if Fin were dancing down the river.

At Iron Canyon the river narrowed between steep black rock faces. The water churned and boiled, forcing its way through. Fin was definitely on board for this one as Darwin confidently piloted the raft through what Simon Fraser and his men had portaged.

Safely through the canyon, Darwin maneuvered the raft into a quiet backwater. He apologized to Fin for this little sightseeing trip but just up from the shore there were some amazing petroglyphs that, in his opinion, could not be missed.

With the raft secured to a fallen tree, Fin shed his flippers and the party of adventurers made their way up the boulder bank to one particularly big rock

JOURNAL

Monday [Sunday] June 5, 1808.

*F*ine weather. In the night the water lowered about two feet. This was an agreeable circumstance. We were off at 5. Good going; a strong current and many rapids in our favour. At 9, we landed at the head of a dangerous place [the Iron Rapids, between Riske Creek and the Chilcotin River]. The river here, which does not exceed thirty yards in breadth, passes between two precipices, and is turbulent, noisy, and awful to behold! The carrying place is about a mile long; the ground rough; but there is a beaten path. However the men took five horses to transport the baggage across, yet were much harassed with fatigue.

Simon Fraser *Letters & Journals, 1806-1808*, ed. W. Kaye Lamb (Toronto: MacMillan, 1960), 73.

tucked among the others. What first appeared as random markings began to take shape the longer Fin looked at them. Chiseled out of the stone with a primitive sharp tool, possibly made of obsidian,* was the outline of what appeared to be a person on horseback. Another image resembled a bighorn sheep like the ones they had seen looking down at them from the cliffs just before the rapids. Still others looked like etchings of hoof prints. They were all mysteriously beautiful.

Half an hour later Fin was back in the water, his head spinning with the power of the images and the sacred nature of the place. The river soon opened up and the current ran smooth and steady, helping him along his way. Knowing this part of the river as well as he did, Darwin let the raft drift without running the motor. The day was hot and still and the crew took turns tumbling overboard into the cool water. Buoyed up by their red life jackets they drifted with the current or swam a few strokes alongside Fin. The landscape was breathtakingly beautiful—dry sagebrush country dotted with majestic Ponderosa pines that clung to the steep banks where golden grasses waved in the gentle breeze.

They soon reached the mouth of the Chilcotin River flowing in from the west, its clear turquoise water mixing with the murky Fraser. As Fin took one of his short breaks along side the raft, Darwin pointed out the largest California

---

*Obsidian is a hard volcanic glass traded among the native peoples of North America for use as tools, blades, arrowheads and decorative objects. Today obsidian is used in some surgical scalpels, having a cutting edge many times sharper than steel.

Bighorn Sheep Reserve in North America and beyond it, on the south side of the Chilcotin, the site of a once thriving Shuswap village. It had been an important trading centre for First Nations people until the smallpox epidemic of 1863 killed most of the villagers. The few that had survived were later struck down by influenza in 1918. Nothing remained of the village.

Threatening clouds began to form behind them to the north as Fin and the raft moved downriver beyond the Gang Ranch Bridge. The wind picked up, the sky grew darker and distant claps of thunder bounced off the surrounding hills. Getting closer and closer, the storm chased them all the way to their next campsite at a place called the Cathedrals. The rain pelted down and the wind howled. With great difficulty they managed to pitch their tents and secure the kitchen area with a big tarp as the force of the mountain storm hurled upon them. Thunder rolled through the hills, shaking the ground with its roar. Bolts of lightening sliced the dark storm sky. Rain pummeled their tents and pooled in the sandy depressions of the campsite. And then, almost as quickly as it had started, it was over, at least for the moment.

The storm moved rapidly down the valley as the skies above them cleared. Across the river on the eastern bank, the golden glow of the late afternoon sun shone brilliantly on an amazing wall of naturally sculpted rock that had been carved away over hundreds of years by wind, rain and sand. From a distance it looked just like the spires of the old European cathedrals.

EXPLORATIONS

The tail end of the storm dropped more rain overnight, but the crew woke to blue sky and a warm breeze funneling down the valley. Since all their gear was soaked through, Darwin announced a later than usual departure to let things dry out a little. This gave Fin time to hike up the steep slopes behind the campsite. He followed paths made by the bighorn sheep around or through the many gullies carved out by run-off from rain and melting snow. Between these gullies meadows of golden grasses rippled in the drying breeze. They looked deceivingly soft and inviting, but hidden among them were vicious cacti, their spines so sharp they could pierce the sole of a shoe.

Fin very carefully climbed higher. The warm air was deliciously scented with sage from the woody shrubs pruned back by grazing bighorns. Some very old bushes had trunks thicker than baseball bats, all twisted and gnarled by the harsh conditions. From his bird's-eye view the raft and campsite were mere specks in the vast landscape. Fin was finally seeing the river as if from the eyes of the eagles that soared above him as he swam. Like the sheep tracks he had been following, the river carved its way south through sand and silt and rock, taking the path of least resistance. He was excited to see the course he and the river would follow that day.

Fin felt so good to be exercising like this. The heat of the sun and the exertion of the climb made him sweat in a way he never experienced in the river. He climbed for the better part of an hour until he saw the sun finally begin to hit the campsite far below, a sign that it was time to head back. Their gear would be drying out quickly and Darwin itching to get back on the water.

Breakfast was ready when he returned and the crew busy packing up. The sky was crystal clear with no sign of any more storms. Day Fourteen promised to be another idyllic but hot one on the river. As Darwin pumped up the raft's pontoons, he cautioned the others to tie everything down really tight in preparation for French Creek Rapids. He told Fin he could swim for about an hour but then they would haul him out for some big waves that would make them all wish they had on wetsuits too.

With Fin on board the crew raced through the canyon, bucking the huge waves and getting as wet as Darwin had promised. And then, once again, the river grew tamer and Fin slipped back into the water, stroking rhythmically on towards Big Bar.

Along the way, the crew saw increasing evidence of abandoned mining activity and, with Darwin's approval, they persuaded Fin to take his lunch break on shore so they could explore what looked like the trenches of a ravaged battlefield. Mounded ridges of clean smooth rocks lay in rows across the wide riverbanks. Scattered between were huge piles of tailings, the rocky refuse

JOURNAL

FRIDAY [THURSDAY], JUNE 9, 1808.

At 7 A.M. our arms and every thing being in due order, we embarked and [a] few hours after arrived at Rapide Couverte [French Bar Canyon]. Here [the] channel contracts to about forty yards, and is inclosed by two precipices of great heighth [height], which bending towards each other make it narrower above than below. The water which rolls down this extraordinary passage in tumultuous waves and with great velocity had a tremendous appearance.

It being absolutely impossible to carry the canoes by land, yet sooner than to abandon them, all hands without hesitation embarked, as it were a corp perdu [a corps perdu: i.e., recklessly] upon the mercy of this Stygian tide. Once engaged the die was cast, and the great difficulty consisted in keeping the canoes in the medium, or fil d'eau [current], that is to say, clear of the precipice on one side, and of the gulphs formed by the waves on the other. However, thus skimming along like lightning, the crews cool and determined, followed each other in awful silence. And [when] we arrived at the end we stood gazing on our narrow escape from perdition.

Simon Fraser *Letters & Journals, 1806-1808*, ed. W. Kaye Lamb (Toronto: MacMillan, 1960), 75–76.

from the miners' search for gold. A dirt road ran into the site, and at the end, a beautiful old red truck was parked. Darwin told them it was the old Johnston Mine, an abandoned placer mine that had been active until quite recently.

Exploring the area, the crew were drawn towards what appeared to be the entrance to an old mine shaft dug into the sandy bank above the truck. A door rested slightly ajar inviting them to push it open, the rusted squeaky hinges announcing their entry to anyone or anything that might be inside. As their eyes adjusted to the darkness of the windowless space, they saw that it was a room, once lived in, not a mine shaft. Carefully, they stepped in further, the cool dank air a welcome relief from the heat of the mid-day sun. An old wire-framed bed stood on one side and on the other was an upturned packing crate topped with the solidified flow of melted candle wax. A few empty tin cans had been kicked into the corner along with one stiff old leather glove and a sweat-stained baseball cap.

Meanwhile, Fin sat under the shade of one of the few trees on the riverbank, eating his veggie sandwich. Between bites he absentmindedly sifted sand and pebbles through his fingers while watching an eagle perched opposite him, suspecting that it too was thinking about the salmon swimming up the river. As the sun filtered gently through the leaves above, something in the sand sparkled brightly, immediately drawing his attention away from the river and the eagle. It was fine and shiny, just like gold dust. Fin instantly began imagining how a discovery of gold would help pay for his swim until Darwin's piercing whistle broke his reveries. Back at the raft the others assured him it was nothing but 'fool's gold.'

Downriver at Big Bar, the crew stopped to replenish their supplies of drinking water just as the reaction ferry was landing, carrying a small truck loaded with freshly cut hay. They were heartily welcomed by the ferry operator who was used to seeing river rafts but certainly not such an odd looking creature as he now saw windmilling its way towards him. Like an eager seal Fin slipped out of the water and up onto the bank to join the others. As he listened to Fin's story, the ferryman realized this guy wasn't so crazy after all but really cared about the life and the health of the great river. He would have happily kept the group there all afternoon, feeding them fresh green beans and tomatoes from his garden and telling them stories of the area but, as usual, the river beckoned.

Stroke by stroke Fin moved leisurely downstream for another couple of hours, arriving at Leon Creek campsite in the early evening. As darkness fell and they were all sharing their impressions of the day around the dying embers of their campfire, a full moon slipped up into the night sky from behind the mountains flanking the eastern bank of the river. Magnificently silhouetted in its centre was a lone pine tree precariously rooted on the highest peak. The perfection of that moment silenced everyone.

TARP TOWN

That night they all slept under the stars. Captain Darwin stretched out on his 'ship' and the rest laid out their sleeping bags around the campfire. One crew member saw ten shooting stars, another watched the moon disappear behind the Coast Mountains while another counted bighorn sheep until he nodded off. The bubbling songs of nearby Leon Creek lulled Fin into instant sleep.

The next morning everyone awoke peacefully, ready for another day of thrills, excitement and potential danger. Darwin again cautioned the crew to tie down the packs, boxes and equipment really tight in preparation for some more exciting water ahead. Fin swam for a short while until they came to the Power Line Rapids which were as big as had been forewarned ... and very

Hoo... Hoo...

thrilling. The ride through these dangerous waters was bumpy and wet, but with the help of the big motor and Darwin's skill the raft made the passage with relative ease.

It wasn't long before they reached Moran Canyon where the Fraser becomes very narrow and the high rock walls on either side squeeze the water through at tremendous speed. The river has cut so deep into the canyon that there are no rapids, but the whirlpools have such tremendous force that they could easily suck down a swimmer who would never surface for another breath.

It was at this point that Simon Fraser was forced to head overland.

SIMON FRASER'S
JOURNAL

SATURDAY [FRIDAY], JUNE 10, 1808.
[near Leon Creek]

*T*his morning sent two men to examine the water. At 10 they returned and confirmed the report of the natives that the River was impracticable. In Consequence we immediately set to work, erected a scaffold for the Canoes where we placed them under a shade of branches to screen the gum from the sun, and such other articles as we could not carry along we buried in the Ground.

Simon Fraser *Letters & Journals, 1806-1808*, ed. W. Kaye Lamb (Toronto: MacMillan, 1960), 77.

As the raft glided swiftly through the canyon, Darwin raised his bottle of water to Fin and the crew and together they toasted the salmon that had played such a huge role in saving the Fraser from being dammed. Back in the 70's there had been a plan to build an enormous hydroelectric dam in Moran Canyon. It would have flooded the valley all the way upstream to Quesnel, and if that had happened neither the salmon nor Fin would have been making their separate journeys.

Fin was on the raft more than he was in the river that morning. He actually didn't mind too much because the scenery was so dramatic and so very different from what he saw while swimming. A couple of bighorn sheep were spotted staring down at the raft and its occupants from a high rocky ledge. And then the eagles! There seemed to be more and more of them perched in trees or soaring high above them as they approached the Bridge River Rapids. A few fish camps appeared on the shore as the canyon walls gave way to craggy outcroppings of granite. Occasionally, a salmon leapt out of the water on its journey north, happy perhaps, to have successfully made it this far, having conquered some very serious rapids and avoided the nets and hooks of some very serious fishermen.

Darwin gently guided the raft towards shore on river right. It was time for everyone but him to get off and take a walk through 'Tarp Town'. With the raft secured to the shore, Fin and the crew jumped off and headed towards the footpath that Darwin pointed out, leaving the captain to do his final check before heading into the rapids. The Bridge River Rapids are so big and so dangerous that no passengers are ever allowed to ride through them. Darwin alone would take the raft down while Fin and the others watched from the shore.

As they moved along the path the number of fish camps increased, dotting both sides of the river with their bright orange and blue tarps. An old woman of the Bridge River Band waved them over, perhaps as curious about them as they were about her. She laughed at the sight of Fin in his wetsuit and thought he looked like a big frog out of water. After satisfying her curiosity about why he was dressed that way and what he was doing, she welcomed them all to her drying shed, a simple wooden structure covered with a tarp. Hanging from the rafters inside were rows of salmon fillets drying in the hot wind that blew like a furnace blast through the canyon. She ripped some strips off a curling red fillet and offered them a taste. Not being a flesh eater but wishing to respect the old woman's friendly gesture Fin took the slightest nibble and had to confess it was rather delicious!

The old woman agreed with him and happily told the visitors how her people had been fishing this way for hundreds of years, taking what fish they needed for food and letting the rest of the salmon carry on up the river to spawn. She pointed to the people fishing from the rocks below and explained how they still caught fish in the traditional way, often in big hand-held dip nets. The salmon were then carried up to her where she cleaned and filleted each one. Before being hung up to dry, each fillet was scored across the grain,

cutting the rich flesh to the skin but not through it. Sadly, she told them, the wasps would soon get so bad that she would have to stop drying the fish and begin to smoke, can, freeze or salt them instead.

They all watched Darwin deftly guide the raft through the foaming rapids. It was with a great deal of care and a bit of a prayer that he plotted his route, counting on the motor as well as his years of experience to help him through. Big licks of water rose up several meters, threatening to turn or flip the raft. The bow pointed skywards, but Darwin held a steady course. At one crucial moment it looked as if the raft came fearfully close to the rock wall on the far bank, but then, in the next moment, it shot over the last of the rapids into the smoother waters below. Darwin circled the raft in towards the flat rock where Fin and the crew, as well as a few onlookers, stood watching and waiting. He was dripping wet, grinning from ear to ear and wishing he could take the raft back up and do it all over again.

The crew and Fin hopped on board and drifted with the current while they ate their lunch, waiting for the river to widen out and calm down. By this time Fin had reached a slow simmer inside his wetsuit and finally, as the river began to open out above Lillooet, Darwin gave him the okay signal. Back in the water, his body drank in the coolness as, stroke by stroke, he continued downriver.

Lillooet was once a hub of trading routes for First Nations people. Early European settlers and gold seekers called it mile zero of the Cariboo Wagon Road that went north to Soda Creek and south to Yale. Today Lillooet continues to serve as a junction town with highways, railroads and rivers converging here only to spread out again in their various directions. After seven days on the river since leaving Prince George, surrounded for the most part by the ever-changing natural beauty of the landscape, the sight of the city came as a shock to Fin. Lego-like houses sat above the railroad tracks running parallel to the highway, and only a few trees were to be seen. Long freight trains snaked along the west

bank hauling
containers of
coal, wheat,
passengers
and other cargo.

A little
further on the
raft was buzzed
by a couple of
noisy jet boats out
on the river for a high-
speed tour, their paying
passengers screaming
with nervous delight.
Darwin kept the raft very close to Fin as the
mood of the river changed once again.

Leaving the noise and activity behind, it was a short
gentle swim to Riley Creek where a lone cow grazed happily on the grassy
flat lands above the riverbank. Initially, the animal seemed unperturbed by
the approaching raft, but when Fin hauled himself out of the water, the cow
immediately took off, tail swishing, to join the rest of the herd out of sight on
the far side of the barbed wire. And, of course, before leaving, it left a fresh
cow patty to join the many other sun-baked plops scattered about the site. So,
it was with particular care that the team members selected their tent sites that
evening among the alder and fruiting hawthorn.

A short distance up the hill, surrounded by Pondersoa pines, the crew was
delighted to find a very respectable outhouse. There was no need that night
to unload and set up 'the groover,' the increasingly heavy and increasingly
malodorous portable toilet they carried with them and the one job they all

joked about and liked the least.

The hot wind they had experienced earlier blowing through Bridge River was still with them. As the sun sank in the western sky, the evening breezes moved from hot to warm and gradually, as darkness fell, a welcomed coolness embraced them. They ate an exceptional dinner of fresh salmon grilled over an open fire, a gift from the old woman at the fish camp. After the busyness of Lillooet, the jet boats and more human activity than they had seen in days, there was a communal sense of contentment and pleasure in the tranquility around them. An owl hooted in the distance as the rising moon lit up the night sky.

TRAIN WRECKS

During the night a light but steady rain fell, refreshing the parched landscape. However, by the time the sun peeked over the hills to the east, rousting Fin from his dampened tent, the skies had completely cleared.

The warm morning breezes were beginning to heat up as Fin set off on Day Sixteen. He swam rhythmically and easily through the water, avoiding the whirlpools that the raft spun in and out of as it quietly floated downstream just ahead of him. On a couple of occasions, when the river became particularly gnarly, Darwin called Fin onto the raft and they all rode through the rapids together.

About midday they reached the mouth of the Stein River where it empties into the Fraser from the west. Its waters, usually clear and blue, were muddied with branches, small trees and upturned, twisted roots. What the team had experienced as a gentle rain the night before must have been a raging storm higher up in the mountains, causing a lot of runoff to carry so much natural debris down into the river. On occasion, travelers have been ordered off the Fraser after a big storm, but Darwin felt confident that there wasn't enough litter in the water to be a serious threat to either Fin or the raft. He did, however, ask everyone to keep a particularly watchful eye on the river ahead. He did not want Fin or the motor to get snagged by floating roots or branches.

Further downstream at Lytton, an even greater river runs into the murky Fraser. The Thompson River, named by Simon Fraser for the explorer David Thompson, is the largest tributary of the Fraser, flowing into it through the dry Interior Plateau to the east. Unlike the Fraser, the Thompson's journey takes it through several lakes, slowing its flow long enough for it to drop much of its accumulated silt and sediment, keeping the water clear and green.

It was down the Thompson River that the other group of Overlanders traveled in 1862 from Tête Jaune Cache to Fort Kamloops. Anticipating the Fraser to be too dangerous, thirty-two of them chose the Thompson route in the hopes of a safer journey to the goldfields. Augustus Schubert, his pregnant wife Catherine, the only woman on the expedition, and their three young children were amongst those who chose the Thompson route, but their trip proved to be no less arduous or dangerous than the Fraser River experience. After forty-two days of grueling travel, the Schubert family arrived at Fort Kamloops just in the nick of time for Catherine to give birth to a healthy baby girl!

Today, the lower Thompson is a favourite for white water adventurers who paddle their rubber rafts or kayaks through wild stretches of foaming water. As Fin swam through the mixing of these two great rivers, a couple of rafting groups had just completed their exciting river descent and were singing and laughing and giving Fin a 'thumbs up' as he carried on down the Fraser and they returned to dry land.

JOURNAL

MONDAY [SUNDAY], JUNE 19, 1808.
[near Lytton]

After having remained some time in this village, the principal chief invited us over the river. We crossed, and He received us at the water side, where, assisted by several others, he took me by the arms and conducted me in a moment up the hill to the camp where his people were sitting in rows, to the number of twelve hundred; and I had to shake hands with all of them.

Simon Fraser *Letters & Journals, 1806-1808*, ed. W. Kaye Lamb (Toronto: MacMillan, 1960), 87.

Lytton is a busy town with highways and railroad tracks crisscrossing both rivers. Canada's two transcontinental rail lines, the CNR and the CPR, converge here to follow the Fraser on its southward journey. Lytton also marks the northern limit of the Cascade Mountain Range that extends all the way south to California, and it is the beginning of the great Fraser Canyon. In 1808 Simon Fraser also found this to be a bustling area and was received here by more people than he had seen in months.

At Siska, a few kilometers downstream from Lytton, twin bridges crisscross the Fraser where the rail lines trade sides, a curious result of corporate expansion and difficult terrain. Even as he swam, Fin was aware of the screeching of metal wheels on metal tracks and the clickity click rhythm of the seemingly endless stream of long trains carrying grain and potash from the prairies and coal and lumber from B.C. out to the port of Vancouver.

A little further down the river, Fin was rapidly approaching a great heap of twisted metal crumpled at the bottom of the steep canyon wall. Since it was time for his lunch break he clambered aboard the raft and listened as Darwin recounted the story of the train wreck they were floating by, alluding to the many others that have and continue to occur. Lives were often lost and the wrecks left where they fell, slowly oozing their cargoes into the river.

Darwin continued with the story of the silk train that derailed just east of Yale on September 21, 1927. Five of her ten precious carloads spilled into the Fraser, the brightly coloured silk floating down the river, draping itself on rocks or washing up on sand bars. They called it the 'million dollar train wreck' and apparently a lot of locals went silk fishing very successfully that day.

The 'silkers,' as they were called, were the express trains that carried nothing but Chinese silk from the port of Vancouver to New York. At that time silk was so incredibly valuable that it was insured by the hour. The faster it got across the country the less it cost the shipper. These special silk trains sped non-stop to New York, traveling as fast as possible. All other trains, even those carrying royalty, were shunted to sidings to let the 'silkers' pass.

The remainder of the day's swim was thrilling but difficult. The canyon became so deep in places it blocked out the sun, except when it was directly overhead. In a moment of relative calm, Fin rolled onto his back and gazed up at the massive cliff faces rising vertically on either side of the river. High above him, backlit by a blue sky delicately swept with light cirrus clouds, an eagle soared. It rose on the currents of warm air, using the updrafts much as the salmon used the river currents and back eddies to their advantage. Fin wondered if the eagle saw him as anything more than an insignificant speck on the swiftly moving river.

There were many dangerous wave sections that afternoon, and Fin took his queues from Darwin as to which rapids were safe to swim and which ones must be ridden through on the raft. Whether in or out of the water it was an exciting passage for all.

Late in the afternoon the river widened out as they approached the Nahatlatch flowing in from the west. Tired and wet, Fin was directed to shore where the team made camp not far from the busy rail line running through the trees just behind them.

SILK DREAMS

Throughout the night, long freight trains rumbled north on the tracks behind the campsite. As they crossed the nearby bridge spanning the Nahatlatch, the rhythmic clatter of their metal wheels became a grinding squeal that echoed into the canyon below.

Just before dawn Fin dreamed that he became wrapped in a length of soft bright red silk that pulled him down under the water. There, on the river bottom, he saw a boxcar that must have rolled down the embankment. The baggage door had burst open spilling out its contents of brightly coloured silk, the very silk that enshrouded him. A school of salmon worked the bales with their noses and fins, freeing the tightly bound fabric. Long colourful ribbons rippled downstream as the salmon wove their way over and under them. The silk seemed to carry Fin along, allowing him to swim with the salmon. Big fish swam upstream towards him, their bodies already beginning to change shape and colour. Smaller salmon swam along beside him, heading out to sea to feed and grow. The river rocks below were washed smooth by the strong current and as Fin reached down to touch them, he suddenly felt short of breath. He struggled for air. The beautiful dream was turning into a nightmare. He didn't think he could hold his breath any longer. And then, a loud train whistle gave him hope that he was nearing the surface. His lungs were about to burst as he threw off the small pillow that had been covering his face. With a big sigh and a very deep breath of the fresh morning air, he shook himself awake, ready to start a new day.

This was their day to go through the famous Hell's Gate. Every year thousands of visitors cross the deep canyon on the footbridge or take the airtram to the other side. The more intrepid tourists shoot the rapids with a professional rafting company. No one would dare to swim through this aqua madness of massive whirlpools whose centrifugal force could suck a swimmer down forty meters or more. Nevertheless, several reporters had asked Fin if he would be swimming through Hell's Gate. What a news story that would have made!

JOURNAL

MONDAY [SUNDAY], JUNE 26, 1808.
[in the Fraser Canyon]

I have been for a long period among the Rocky Mountains, but have never seen any thing equal to this country, for I cannot find words to describe our situation at times. We had to pass where no human being should venture. Yet in those places there is a regular footpath impressed, or rather indented, by frequent traveling upon the very rocks. And besides this, steps which are formed like a ladder, or the shrouds of a ship, by poles hanging to one another and crossed at certain distances with twigs and withes [tree boughs], suspended from the top to the foot of precipices, and fastened at both ends to stones and trees, furnished a safe and convenient passage to the Natives – but we, who had not the advantages of their experience, were often in imminent danger, when obliged to follow their example.

Simon Fraser *Letters & Journals, 1806-1808*, ed. W. Kaye Lamb (Toronto: MacMillan, 1960), 96.

The early morning air was fresh and clear. A murder of crows cackled non-stop in the trees behind the campsite as more trains rumbled past. Fin couldn't shake a peculiar melancholy that had come over him. Crows are scavengers and with the exception of Bridge River, he had not seen any until now. He associated them with human populations, their food and their garbage. Sadly he realized that the 'wilderness' part of his odyssey was behind him.

Fin took a few extra moments with his morning ritual, asking the river for its protection. He was both excited and a little nervous about the day ahead. The canyon down to and including Hell's Gate is so narrow and so deep that powerful whirlpools and mighty boils make most of this part of the river impossible to swim. Darwin was very familiar with this stretch and knew the importance of the motor that would power them through the treacherous rapids. Fin trusted the captain's judgment completely and knew that Darwin would only let him swim when it was safe.

Fin was in and out of the water for about an hour before he was joined by two rafts of excited day-trippers just below Boston Bar. With the flotilla of rafts in front of him Fin stroked on until he could tell by Darwin's alert body language that the order was soon coming to get onto the raft. Everyone was dressed in rain gear and ready for a thrilling ride. In fact, some of the rapids above Hell's Gate were so exciting that the actual passage through the 'gate of hell' turned out to be anticlimactic. Tourists on the footbridge waved energetically and shouted greetings in many different languages, most of which could not be heard over the roar of the water and the shrieks of those on board as the rafts hurtled past.

Darwin knew the river down to Yale extremely well, but he always kept a vigilant eye on the fast flowing water ahead. The current was really strong, and he needed to anticipate the conditions soon enough to get Fin safely out of the water. As they all motored through the rapids at Sailor Bar, a huge wall of water washed right over the raft. Even Darwin at the back got drenched, but came out the other side wearing a big satisfied smile.

The scenery was spectacular. The high rocky banks of the canyon were increasingly topped with Douglas fir and cedar, a change from the ponderosa pines and sage of the dry lands further north. The canyon they traveled through was dark and cool and the dancing white water tumbled, sometimes thundered, downstream. A few native fishermen along the shore waved friendly greetings if they had a free hand. Occasionally a salmon leapt high into the air. Hungry eagles were on watch from the treetops.

While they traveled Darwin recounted some of the many stories of the river and the area. If Fin was out of the water long enough he might catch an entire story such as that of the sternwheeler, the S. S. Skuzzy. She was built in Spuzzum, just north of Yale, for Andrew Onderdonk, the contractor who oversaw the building of the CPR. Getting supplies and materials to his construction camps by land had proved to be both expensive and unreliable, so he built a ship that would carry the goods between Boston Bar and Lytton. In the spring of 1882, the 'Skuzzy' was launched and then had to be brought upstream through all the rapids including Hell's Gate. It took several tries, three different captains, an amazingly powerful winch on her bow deck and 125 Chinese labourers hauling on a separate cable to pull her up through Hell's Gate and then two weeks more to get her to Lytton.

And, as if that undertaking wasn't crazy enough, twenty years before the Skuzzy, an enterprising individual had brought twenty-one camels to Yale, believing they would adapt well as baggage animals on the Cariboo Road. However, it turned out that the sight and smell of these exotic critters terrified the mules and packhorses sharing the narrow trail. They refused to pass the camels and chaos reigned. To make matters even worse, it was soon discovered that the rocky terrain cut their spongy feet to pieces. Poor beasts! They were set free and left to roam in the dry interior, the last of the line dying in 1905.

As the raft approached Yale, Darwin pointed out a high peak on the east side of the river, a sacred mountain to the First Nations people of the area. It

was said that during the time of the Great Flood, as the rains fell and the river rose, the people of the village saved themselves by tying their canoes to a big rock on the mountaintop. That same rock had recently been blasted away by engineers since it was thought to be an impending threat to the railway below.

Fin swam into Yale, fighting the back current near the shore where a number of people were milling about having just finished a gentle float down the river. As he hauled his weary but exhilarated body up onto the beach an elderly lady, a little shaky on her legs, asked for his hand to help steady her on the soft sand. She was totally oblivious to the strenuous swim that Fin had just completed. He smiled, a twinkle in his blood-shot eyes, as he took her hand and together they walked up the beach to the van waiting to take the seniors back home.

YALE to VANCOUVER

LOWER FRASER

BEYOND HOPE

Today Yale is a quiet little village with a population of about 200 residents sandwiched between the Trans-Canada Highway on one side and the CPR tracks and Fraser River on the other. But in 1858, at the height of Gold Fever, the town's residents numbered as many as 20,000 when it was said to be the largest city north of San Francisco and west of Chicago. At that time, Yale was the inland terminus for steamboat navigation traveling up from the coast and the starting point of the Cariboo Wagon Road for those continuing north. Many of the miners stayed in Yale and panned the gold-rich river bars above and below the town while others moved further north. There was a thriving Chinatown at the north end, up the road from the hotels, saloons and outfitters that serviced the miners and other travelers. Some called it "the wickedest little settlement in B.C." Later, the construction of the Canadian Pacific Railroad in the 1880's brought another boom to Yale and its population soared to 50,000. Hardly anything remains of those early days, except for the Church of St. John the Divine built in 1863, the oldest church on the B.C. mainland.

The sky was heavy over Yale on the morning of Day Eighteen and threatening dark clouds obscured the sacred mountaintop across the river. The temperature had dropped several degrees and the crew was somewhat subdued. Perhaps their change of mood was brought on by the hint of fall in the air and the fact that they would be leaving the canyon and the long north-south stretch of the mighty river they had been traveling together since leaving Prince George nine days earlier. After a short swim downriver to Hope, they would turn west to follow the Lower Fraser for the final leg of their journey out to the coast.

A few kilometers into the day's swim, the river swung out around a big gravel bar where the gold rush had actually started. It was named Hill's Bar for the first prospector to find gold on the river in 1858. There were a few small rapids to swim through but nothing serious, and it took just a little over two hours to reach Hope. As they moved out of the canyon seagulls circled above, and a couple of majestic great blue herons stood statue-like, patiently fishing in the quiet shallow waters at the edge of the river. The sharp whistle of an osprey circling high above drew Fin's eyes skywards to watch the great bird tuck its wings, plummet straight into the water and reappear with a fish clutched in its talons.

Beyond Hope and heading west the river gradually widened out. The heavy clouds began to break up and a cool breeze blew with increasing strength. By late morning, Fin was swimming against a ferocious westerly wind funneling up the widening valley between the steep mountains on either side. The water was choppy with white caps breaking in front of him, sometimes right over him. The strong wind blew spray from his stroking arms back into his face. He felt as if he was making no headway at all. But, keeping an eye on the shore to mark his progress, he could see that the current remained strong, propelling him forward at a good clip in spite of the wind.

During their lunch break the wind calmed and the sun began to break through the clouds, warming them all in both body and spirit. The mood of the river as well as that of the team had changed dramatically. Looking west, the landscape opened up with the Coast Mountain Range to the north and the Cascades to the south pushing back and away from the river. The canyon had been spectacular but very claustrophobic and now the feeling was increasingly open and expansive, as if the coast itself was drawing them onwards.

Back in the water and several kilometers beyond Hope, Fin could see the glacier on Mount Cheam which had always signified, for him, the gateway to Vancouver. His heart gave a little leap of excitement at the thought of the end of his epic swim. His voice of reason, however, quickly reminded him of the four long days of swimming still to go as he vigorously picked up his stroke.

A few recreational fishermen began to appear on the gravel banks, hoping to catch some of the migrating salmon that occasionally leapt out of the water and twisted into the air. In the distance speeding cars and trucks could be heard on the highway along with the rumbling of passing trains.

That night they made camp on a small island a few kilometers above Agassiz. In fact, it wasn't really an island but a big gravel bar that had been built up over the years by the river depositing enough gravel and silt to allow a few trees to grow. Its pebble beach was long and smooth, and its silty banks were marked by the footprints of Canada geese and deer. As the evening sun sank towards the horizon the team was wrapped in a warm rosy glow.

SASQUATCH

In the early morning Fin went for a run down the long flat pebble beach. It felt so good to really stretch his legs. Lifting his arms skywards he gave a joyous howl, exhilarated by the wide, open valley. Until now he had not realized just how confining the magnificent canyon had been.

As Darwin tied the gear onto the raft he sniffed the air and sensed a change in the weather. The gentle morning breeze was gradually shifting, and he felt like it could blow up into something big. Perhaps Fin's swim that day might not be the easy float he had anticipated.

Plunging in, it didn't take Fin long to warm up as he stroked confidently through the increasingly choppy water. He hoped the morning headwind was not a pattern he would battle for the remainder of the trip. As the river widened and the valley opened out even more, the current weakened, the wind strengthened and the swimming felt just as hard as it had the day before. Fishermen lined the shore and a few small recreational boats bounced through the curling whitecaps.

Near the mouth of the Harrison River, the spiny back of an enormous white sturgeon suddenly broke the surface of the water. Loud exclamations arose from the raft. The giant fish must have been a couple of meters long and one of the biggest Darwin had ever seen in all his years on the river. An old river guy had once told him about a sturgeon that was caught further downriver near New Westminster back in 1897. It weighed over 600 kilograms and was probably more than 100 years old. Besides being the largest freshwater fish in North America, white sturgeon are thought to be as old or maybe even older than dinosaurs.

Disappointed to have missed the rare sighting, Fin resumed swimming, carefully scanning the surface of the water with the hope that the sturgeon might reappear. Instead, all he saw was a seal, the first of many he would encounter as he moved closer to the coast.

A little further on, everyone was on the raft having a lunch of veggie wraps. Between bites oozing with mayonnaise, Darwin announced that they were drifting through Sasquatch country, and as he pulled out an old newspaper clipping he asked if anyone believed that these creatures actually existed.

WHAT IS IT?

A STRANGE CREATURE CAPTURED ABOVE YALE

Yale, B.C., July 3rd, 1882. (stet)   In the immediate vicinity of No. 4 tunnel situated some twenty miles above this village, are bluffs of rock which have hitherto been unsurmountable, but on Monday morning last were successfully scaled by Mr. Onderdonk's employees on the regular train from Lytton. Assisted by Mr. Costerton, the British Columbia Express Company's messenger, and a number of gentlemen from Lytton and points east of that place, who, after considerable trouble and perilous climbing, succeeded in capturing a creature half man and half beast. "Jacko," as the creature has been called by his capturers, is something of the gorilla type

A British Columbia Gorilla

standing about four feet seven inches in height and weighing 127 pounds. He has long, black, strong hair and resembles a human being with one exception, his entire body, excepting his hands, (or paws) and feet are covered with glossy hair about one inch long. His fore arm is much longer than a man's fore arm, and he possesses extraordinary strength, as he will take hold of a stick and break it by wrenching or twisting it, which no man living could break in the same way. Since his capture he is very reticent, only occasionally uttering a noise which is half bark and half growl. He is, however, becoming daily more attached to his keeper, Mr. George Tilbury, of this place, who proposes shortly starting for London, England, to exhibit him. His favourite food so far is berries, and he drinks fresh milk with evident relish. By advice of Dr. Hannington raw meats have been withheld from Jacko, as the doctor thinks it would have a tendency to make him savage . . .

The article elicited both laughter and some heated discussion as they floated peacefully with the current, now that the wind had died down. All was quiet around them, so quiet in fact that they could hear a gentle, swishing sound as the sandy silt in the river gently brushed against the raft's rubber pontoons. As much as Fin was enjoying the camaraderie and the peacefulness around him, he reluctantly rolled overboard and continued his swim.

Around Chilliwack the river bends through some of the richest farmland in the world. This is the eastern extremity of the alluvial flood plain of the Fraser where rich river sediments have been deposited over centuries. Beyond the flood plain to the south there was once a big shallow lake that stretched between Sumas Mountain to the west and Vedder Mountain further inland. In the 1920's the lake was drained, apparently to get rid of mosquitoes. The result was the addition of over 30,000 acres of very rich farmland, now known as the Sumas Prairie. It actually sits below sea level and continues to rely on the Vedder Canal to keep it well drained.

At this point the river's current was almost non-existent and the rest of the afternoon's swim was slogging and laborious. Fin was reminded of his first days on the river, zigzagging his way through the Rocky Mountain Trench, the current slow and the distances seemingly endless.

Finally the Mission Bridge came into sight with the town of Mission rising on the right, crowned by the tower of Westminster Abbey, a Benedictine monastery built in 1954. A short distance beyond the town, Darwin signaled Fin to head for shore where they set up camp. Only two more nights on the river and how urban it was beginning to feel and look and . . . smell!

TIDAL CURRENTS

No one had noticed the farm access road and rail crossing just behind the trees when they set up camp. Throughout the night a lot of trains went by, and every one of them sounded its warning whistle followed by the annoying 'ding, ding, ding' of the crossing gate. One train even shunted back and forth for what seemed like an hour with the 'ding, ding' going all the time.

The next morning Fin and the others emerged from their tents looking haggard and bleary-eyed. No one had slept well that night, and it was indeed a grumpy beginning to the second to last day on the river. To add to the grumpiness, they found the raft high and dry down on the beach. Darwin had not anticipated that the rhythms of the changing tides would extend this far upriver! But, as frustrating as it was, they all had a good laugh and took their time over breakfast while waiting for the tide to come in and float them on their way.

When they finally got on the river the tide was slack, the water smooth and the swimming easy. More fishermen lined the banks or drifted with the current in their small boats. Not wishing to be snagged as 'the big one,' Fin was careful to stay well away from their lines. Some of the fishermen called out, "Way to go Fin. You're almost there." Fin smiled to himself as he lifted his arm in a friendly wave, happy that the media must be paying some attention to his swim. How else would the fishermen have known his name?

The smells around Fin were changing. From the riverside farms came the sweet and sour aroma of manure, sometimes mixed with the choking stench of chemical fertilizers and herbicides. He could smell gasoline from the motors of the fishermen's runabouts and diesel fumes from the increasing number of commercial trawlers and tugboats on the river. Even the smell of fish tickled Fin's nostrils.

He had to watch carefully where he swam as more and more rogue logs appeared on the water, escapees from the huge booms being towed to an increasing number of sawmills and processing plants. And, he made every effort to avoid the little islets of yellowish foam that floated by. Whatever they were, he didn't fancy swallowing any.

Some distance ahead, Fin saw the Albion ferry carrying cars from one side of the river to the other. It was the only crossing between Mission and the Port Mann Bridge so, even though the early morning rush was over, there was still a line up of cars waiting to be ferried to the other side.

Noticing how quickly he was approaching the ferry, Fin realized the tide had turned again. The ebb tide was now helping to move him along towards the sea. He stopped briefly for his regular energy break and let the others know that he wanted to keep swimming as long as the tide was with him. His lunch could wait. As he swam past the ferry at the Albion dock, the captain gave him

a friendly wave and an encouraging toot of the ship's whistle.

The ebb tide gradually weakened near Haney so Fin joined the others for a quick lunch on the raft. The spicy smell of freshly cut wood, accompanied by the industrial buzz of saws, chains and heavy equipment, filled the air around them as they floated by the local sawmills. A big crane sat perched on a pier like some great monster silhouetted against the craggy Golden Ears of Mount Blanshard to the north. The river was increasingly active with tug boats moving large log booms, smaller vessels that looked like floating tractors herding rogue logs, fish boats, pleasure boats and even a couple of whining Sea-Doos. The energy was thrilling, but a shocking contrast to the general tranquility they had experienced since starting their journey almost three weeks earlier.

When Fin re-entered the water the tide was slack, and he wanted to gain as much distance as possible before it turned again. Up ahead, he could see that the river split and he followed the raft as it passed to the north side of Barnston Island, an agricultural community linked to the mainland on the south by a small ferry.

Joining the increasing river traffic was a Coast Guard boat. It drew alongside the raft, and one of its crew informed Darwin that they would be alerting boats along the way to watch out for the marathon swimmer and his support raft. With all the activity on the river, they were a little worried about Fin's safety.

Around the next bend loomed the familiar sight of the Port Mann Bridge, its bright orange arches distinct against the clear blue sky to the west. Fin knew the plan was to camp on the far side of the bridge, but just as he began thinking of the evening's massage and a well-earned dinner, he felt the increasing resistance of the flood tide moving in, and it was strong. He realized it was likely to take him an hour or two of very hard work before the day's swim ended.

The river that had helped him speed along earlier in the afternoon was now fighting his every stroke. He swam as close to the shore as possible, where the strength of the incoming tide was slightly less, but he still had to stroke with all his might to avoid losing ground. The bridge didn't seem to be getting any closer, and he felt as though he were on a treadmill. The crew sang to him, made jokes and shouted out words of encouragement. The Coast Guard kept up their vigilance, circling back on Fin from time to time, cheering him on. Fin thought of the salmon and their long struggle upriver, occasionally finding a back current to assist them. He thought about their determination and his own to finish his marathon journey. How extraordinary to find himself thinking and feeling like a fish! Purposefully, he counted out his strokes in groups of one hundred. Stroke . . . Stroke . . . Stroke . . . 89 . . . 90 . . . 91. Swimming into the long late afternoon shadows of the Port Mann Bridge, he saw and heard the flood tide breaking around the huge pylons. 28 . . . 29 . . . 30 . . . Keep going.

Soon the raft came alongside and gently nudged him towards the boat ramp that extended from a quickly disappearing beach just a few meters away. Exhausted but smiling, Fin dragged himself out at Maquabeak Park where a cheering crowd awaited. The celebratory reception was almost overwhelming, but all he could think of at that moment was that, after just one more sleep, he would be in his own bed again.

INTO THE CITY

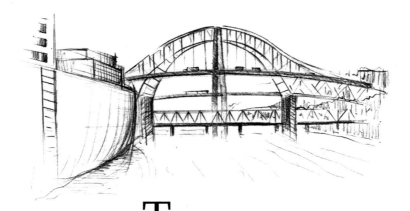

That night there was quite a party in Maquabeak Park. Friends, family and enthusiastic supporters came bearing both food and celebratory greetings. Municipal dignitaries were there to congratulate Fin and to plant a tree in his honour, acknowledging his concern for the environment. The media was also on hand, and journalists were finally becoming very interested in his story now that he was easily accessible and almost at the end of his long swim.

Little Maquabeak Park is situated in the middle of an industrial complex under the north ramp of the Port Mann Bridge. A steady stream of cars and trucks rumbling overhead throughout the night made for less than ideal sleeping conditions. Then, to make matters worse, the night watchman thought they were camping illegally and woke the team about midnight, unaware that they had been given permission to use the site. As the sun rose curious dogs, out with their owners for their early morning watering, nosed the tents and delivered big, wet, friendly kisses to each face that appeared.

Darwin was first to emerge from his tent and was very happy to see his raft still floating and safely secured to the dock at the boat launch. Low tide would not hold them back today. Soon everyone was up and busy preparing for the twenty-first and last day on the river. Fin shook out the sand and silt from his soggy wetsuit before putting it on for the last time. This was one thing he would not miss. Oddly enough, he could not find his fins. Everyone took part in the search for the missing flippers, but they were nowhere to be found and Fin was mightily annoyed. Surely no one would steal his fins unless perhaps as a souvenir in case he became famous one day. Not wanting to waste any more time, he slipped on his neon yellow reserve pair and was comforted by the thought that they might actually be more easily spotted on the busy river.

By 8 a.m. they were off. Soon Fin swam past a big ocean-going freighter docked at the side of the river where it was being loaded with cars crushed into metal pancakes, ready for export to some other place for some other use. He swam past sawmills, some new and brightly painted, some dark and dreary wearing the dirty patina of age and use. Booms were secured in front of the mills where powerful little 'side-winders' manipulated the logs out of the water and onto conveyor belts that carried them up into the mill. There the bark would be shorn off before the logs were moved along to the big saw blade and cut into planks, coming out the other end to be piled and bound, ready for shipment. The remaining sawdust and woodchips were blasted into huge storage piles or loaded directly onto waiting barges to be used as fuel or mulch or to be further processed into particleboard.

The river bustled with activity as Fin swam on. There were fish boats, tugboats, barges, pleasure boats, sightseeing boats, ocean-going freighters, 'river tractors,' kayaks and even the odd canoe. Fin and the crew were very relieved to have the Coast Guard with them again.

The river narrowed as he approached the grouping of three bridges that span the Fraser, the last crossing before it branches into its North and South Arms. The first was a low train bridge that could swivel open to allow large ships to pass through. Just as Fin swam under it the Rocky Mountaineer roared overhead, sounding its horn with a mighty blast that reverberated all around him. Next, came the orange and blue Patullo Bridge that arcs high over the river and carries across cars and trucks. And, just beyond, he swam under the last elegant concrete crossing built for the rapid transit Sky Train that shuttles commuters to and from their urban and suburban destinations.

As he swam past Queen's Quay in New Westminster, shoppers and tourists stopped to wave while an enthusiastic group of school children held up a banner they had made. 'Go Fin. Swim like a fish. You're almost there.' He was so encouraged by the enthusiasm from people he didn't even know, unlike the experience reported by Simon Fraser.

When the river split further downstream, the raft and Fin forked to the right, taking the North Arm under the Queensborough Bridge and around the north side of Lulu Island. Tugs pulling barges and log booms, fish boats and pleasure craft use this arm while the big ocean going vessels travel the wider arm to the south of Richmond. Big warehouse outlets of familiar multi-national businesses appeared on the south bank. Stroke . . . Stroke . . . Tommy Hilfiger! . . . Stroke . . . Stroke . . . Walmart! . . . Stroke . . . Stroke . . . Sleep Country!

As Fin swam through Burnaby, the river once again took on a pastoral nature. Because the municipality had designated this area as a green belt, there was no industry. Trees and grassy banks extended down to the river's edge where herons were patiently fishing and mocking mallards paddled about. Cormorants, the first they had seen, perched on floating logs to dry their outspread wings. Gulls and terns swooped overhead searching competitively

SIMON FRASER'S
JOURNAL

SUNDAY [SATURDAY], JULY 2, 1808.

We proceeded on for two miles, and came to a place where the river divides [at New Westminster] into several channels. Seeing a canoe following us we waited for its arrival. One Indian of that canoe embarked with us and conducted us into the right channel [the North Arm of the Fraser River]. In the meantime several Indians from the village followed in canoes, armed with bows and arrows, clubs, spears &c. Singing a war song, beating time with their paddles upon the sides of the canoes, and making signs and gestures highly inimicable. The one that embarked with us became very unruly singing and dancing, and kicking up the dust. We threatened him with the effect of our displeasure and he was quiet.

This was an alarming crisis, but we were not discouraged; confident of our superiority, at least on the water, we continued.

Simon Fraser *Letters & Journals, 1806-1808*, ed. W. Kaye Lamb (Toronto: MacMillan, 1960), 105.

for food. Occasionally a fish jumped.

The sun was high in the sky. The tide was low and slack, but Fin knew that in a couple of hours he would once again be battling the dreaded flood tide. The very thought spurred him on to cover as much distance as he could before that happened.

He swam to the north of Mitchell Island and on towards the Knight Street Bridge. As he crossed the municipal boundary into the city of Vancouver, the tempo of activity seemed to quicken and big planes roared overhead, flying low as they prepared for landing at Vancouver International Airport. Cars, buses, trucks and tandem trailers sped across the bridge while the river traffic below continued to be heavy. The noise from more sawmills and cement factories added to the cacophonous symphony.

The bombardment on all his senses began to take its toll. Just past Mitchell Island with the Oak Street Bridge in sight, Fin began to feel resistance from the incoming flood tide. With eyes stinging, muscles aching and the bitter taste of both pollution and salt in his mouth, he signaled to the raft that it was time for him to stop for lunch and a rest. Darwin gently nosed the raft up against an abandoned Seaspan barge secured to the remnants of an old wharf. The barge was a thing of dilapidated beauty with its horizontally slatted boards fading into varied hues of red, its metal hull dripping with orange rust, its general decay now the rooting ground for colourful weeds. Against this painterly backdrop they ate their last lunch in silence, watching and listening to the river's multilayered activity.

The planes approaching the airport were so low now that Fin could actually see heads in the oval windows. Tugboats, some with barges in tow, motored by as well as a few trawlers and a couple of speed boats. And then, a seal silently surfaced, fixed its big round eyes directly on Fin and beckoned him back into the water for the last leg of his epic swim.

Big factories lined the north side of the river. The last and the biggest

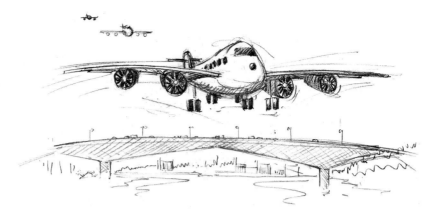

was Ocean Cement, just west of the Oak Street Bridge. Limestone and clay were being carried up a long conveyor belt from barges that had brought the material downstream from quarries the team had passed near Mission. Other conveyor belts and big cranes made the site look like an amusement park of giant slides and roller coasters.

The tide wasn't as strong and the swimming wasn't as difficult as the previous afternoon. Almost before he knew it, Fin was beyond the last bridge, the Arthur Lang Bridge, and was stroking evenly up the north side of Sea Island. On both sides industry soon gave way to green and open spaces and a calm set in over the river. Fish boats and tugs, their bows bearded with old rubber tires, continued to ply the north arm in both directions and seemed to move even more majestically on this pastoral stretch of the river.

The Coast Guard had been with them all day warning those on the river of the marathon swimmer ahead. Now their boat came alongside Fin to ask if he was willing to speak to the media waiting nearby. They had already filmed him swimming back near the Ocean Cement factory, and they would be on hand for his arrival at the Rivers Day celebrations in MacDonald Park but, since he was ahead of schedule and ready for a break, Fin agreed. He swam over to a log boom secured to a cluster of pylons that river folk call a "dolphin" and conducted the interview seated like a large mythical frog on the edge of the boom—good footage, he thought, for the evening's television news.

Half an hour later the camera was still on him as he rolled off the logs and began swimming again. Dogs barked. Their owners waved. Fin could hardly believe his marathon swim was almost over. Twenty-one days on the river. He and the Fraseriffics had become such a close team. He would miss them. He couldn't have done it without them and, as he stroked the final few kilometers, Fin reflected on all the good and all the hard times. Beside him a couple of salmon gracefully arced out of the water, beginning their long journey just as Fin was ending his.

Cheers and whistles pulled him from his reveries. Just a few more strokes and Fin's river journey was over. Eager hands helped him out of the water where he stood facing the chief of the Musqueam Nation at the front of the gathered crowd.

"My name is Finbarr Donnelly. I am 29 years old. I was born in New Westminster. I have come from Tête Jaune Cache, swimming the length of the mighty Fraser River, swimming for the health of the river, swimming for the salmon. I ask your permission to now come on to the traditional lands of the Musqueam Nation."

"Permission granted and welcome."